The SPORTS HEROES Library

Football's
BREAKAWAY BACKS

Nathan Aaseng

Lerner Publications Company • Minneapolis

To Norm

LIBRARY OF CONGRESS CATALOGING IN PUBLICATION DATA

Aaseng, Nathan.
　Football's breakaway backs.

　(The Sports heroes library)
　SUMMARY: Biographies of 10 professional football running backs: O. J. Simpson, Larry Csonka, John Riggins, Franco Harris, Greg Pruitt, Chuck Foreman, Walter Payton, Tony Dorsett, Wilbert Montgomery, and Earl Campbell.

　1. Running backs (Football)—United States—Biography—Juvenile literature. [1. Football players] I. Title.

GV939.A1A16　1980　　796.332′092′2 [B] [920]　　80-16691
ISBN 0-8225-1063-4　(lib. bdg.)

Copyright © 1980 by Lerner Publications Company

All rights reserved. International copyright secured. No part of this book may be reproduced in any form whatsoever without permission in writing from the publisher except for the inclusion of brief quotations in an acknowledged review.

Manufactured in the United States of America

International Standard Book Number: 0-8225-1063-4
Library of Congress Catalog Card Number: 80-16691

2 3 4 5 6 7 8 9 10 90 89 88 87 86 85 84 83 82 81

Contents

	Introduction	5
1	O. J. Simpson	7
2	Larry Csonka	15
3	John Riggins	23
4	Franco Harris	29
5	Greg Pruitt	35
6	Chuck Foreman	43
7	Walter Payton	49
8	Tony Dorsett	55
9	Wilbert Montgomery	60
10	Earl Campbell	67

The Cowboys' Tony Dorsett gets ready to race around a New York Giant defender.

Introduction

From the moment he grabs the handoff, the running back has to think fast. In a split second, he must see if his path is clear and must notice how well his blockers are doing. He also needs to find where the 11 defenders are and know the best way to get past them. And all this must be done while he's running at top speed. How do you teach someone to think that fast? You can't. A great runner knows where to go without thinking about it.

A runner has less to learn about playing his position than most other players. He usually shows the skills he will need as a pro long before he finishes college. Because of this, spotting a top running back is a pro scout's easiest job. When a runner is chosen in the first round of the National Football League (NFL) draft, he almost always becomes a star. In fact, eight of the ten runners in this book were number one draft picks, and each has his own special way of staying a winner. Some make use of brute power. They can bowl over defensive players and drag 1,000 pounds of linemen on their backs for extra yards. Others use speed. They can sprint around or through the line before the defenders even know they have the ball.

But it takes more than power and speed to be a good running back. A good runner must know when to put on a burst of speed and when to lower his head and ram into someone. Many of football's top runners are neither unusually strong or fast, but somehow they know how to give the right fakes so the defender is leaning the wrong way.

Although the running back gets most of the glory, he is very careful to praise his offensive linemen. He knows he could do nothing without fine blocking. A running back needs his big blocking friends to clear the way for him and keep him injury-free. And even with good blocking, a running back still takes a pounding on almost every play. But when he bursts through a wall of tacklers and dashes into the open field, it all seems worthwhile. Each of these runners has done that often enough to be called one of football's breakaway backs.

1
O. J. Simpson

Nearly every football fan has seen Orenthal James Simpson outrun entire defenses for touchdowns. But some of his better runs were seen only by the police. When O. J. was younger, he was the leader of a teenage gang in San Francisco called the "Superiors." More than once, his speed helped to save him from a close call with the police. Fortunately, as he grew older, O. J. found a more useful way to use his running skill. He became such a great running back that he is certain to win a spot in the football Hall of Fame.

O. J. did not always have a runner's strong legs. As a small boy, his legs were so skinny and weak

When he played for the Buffalo Bills, O. J. Simpson was the best running back in football.

he had to wear braces, and kids used to laugh at him. But he loved to run, and his legs grew stronger. As his running skill got better and better, he, unfortunately, got into more and more trouble. His mother did her best to keep O. J. from "running" with his gang and eventually separated him from his trouble-making buddies by sending him to a different high school.

In high school, O. J. began to use his running skills on the football field. Because he played on a losing team, colleges didn't take any interest in him. But O. J. decided he wanted to be a part of the great football team at the University of Southern California and hoped he might be noticed if he played at a small college. So O. J. worked hard on and off the football field at the City College of San Francisco, waiting for a break.

O. J.'s plan worked. After seeing him run at San Francisco, Southern Cal could hardly wait to get him in one of their uniforms. And once they did, they made sure his talent did not go to waste. Starting in 1967, Simpson often carried the ball 40 times in a game! It was not unusual to see him gain over 200 yards in an afternoon. O. J. was also a member of the Southern Cal 440 relay team that set a world record.

Simpson's great running on the football field earned him the Heisman Trophy as college football's top player in 1968. And in 1969 the Buffalo Bills made Simpson the first player to be chosen in the draft.

O. J.'s first problem as a pro was that his head was too big! He had to practice without a helmet until the Bills could find one that would fit him. Buffalo fans thought he had a "big head" in another way, too. Actions such as staying away from training camp until the Bills offered him more money and flying around the country taking care of business deals irritated fans. They also felt they weren't getting their money's worth watching O. J. play. Indeed, until 1972, Simpson was no better than any ordinary pro running back.

Some of the blame for O. J.'s weak start as a pro must go to his coaches. They tried to use him mainly as a blocker and a pass receiver, and this didn't give O. J. many chances to show what he could really do. Meanwhile, the Bills continued to stumble along as football's worst team.

But 1972 brought a change, and Lou Saban took over as coach. He knew Simpson was something

O. J. turns upfield against the Minnesota Vikings.

special. He found linemen who were at their best when blocking on running plays. Then he turned O. J. loose.

Suddenly O. J. began to break away from defenders. In 1972 the Juice, as his teammates called him (short for *Orange Juice*), won his first rushing title. The following year he set off after a goal that no one had dared think about reaching.

It was not enough for him to break Jim Brown's record of 1,863 yards gained in a season. Instead O. J. aimed to top 2,000 yards! To reach his goal, he especially picked on the New England Patriots. In the two games Buffalo played against New England that season, O. J. sped past fallen Patriot defenders for more than 460 yards.

In the last game of the year against the New York Jets, Simpson had a good chance of breaking the record. The fans were wild with hope, but his blockers wanted him to get 2,000 yards even more than the fans did. After each play, they would rush back to the huddle. "More, Juice, more!" they chanted.

In the second half, the sun went down and the snow began to fall. The fans started to shiver. But O. J. kept wearing his short sleeves so he could "feel" where the New York Jet tacklers were. Finally he broke loose for a short gain behind the block of his left tackle. The Bills went wild! The fans went wild! The run gave him 2,003 yards for the year. Following the game, reporters tried to draw the Juice away from everyone so they could interview him. But O. J. would go nowhere without bringing his blockers along.

In 1979 O. J. finished his pro football career with the San Francisco 49'ers.

While playing for the Buffalo Bills, Simpson won two more running titles in 1975 and 1976. Then in 1978 he was traded to his old home team, the San Francisco 49'ers. Before joining the 49'ers, 1974 had been the only year Simpson had managed to reach the play-offs. He hoped San Francisco would help him in his dream of playing in a Super Bowl game. But the 49'ers were poorly managed, and they won only a handful of games in his two years with them.

Though he played most of his career for losing teams, O. J. will always be remembered as a winner. He is the second-leading yard-gainer of all the runners in pro football history. Only injuries during his last years of playing kept him from the chance to beat out Jim Brown for the top spot. Fans will have a hard time forgetting O. J.'s famous sprints down the sidelines for touchdowns or the familiar sunny smile on posters, TV, and in the movies. When he retired in 1979, O. J. Simpson was probably the best-known football player in the United States.

2
Larry Csonka

There was nothing fancy about the way Larry Csonka ran with the football. Old-timers say he reminded them of fullbacks during the early days of the sport. Csonka charged straight ahead with raw power and didn't care how muddy he got or what he ran into. Players who got in his way were in for a blast! The 6-foot, 3-inch, 238-pounder may have been the only runner who ever received a penalty for roughness while carrying the ball. Early in his career, referees blew the whistle on him for swinging his arm too hard at a defensive back.

Larry always enjoyed the rough and tumble life. When he was growing up on a 30-acre farm near Stow, Ohio, he played hard and never worried about any injury less serious than a broken bone. So, of course, the rugged sport of football was

Larry Csonka crushes through the Chicago Bears.

Csonka's idea of a good time, and he started playing at an early age. By eighth grade, he played in the defensive line because he had grown larger than the other boys.

Larry might have stayed a lineman all his life if it hadn't been for a poor kickoff in a high school game. The ball bounced to Larry, who was playing as a blocker. He found he enjoyed the thrill of escaping tacklers. That one carry was all he needed to make up his mind to become a running back.

But when Larry entered Syracuse University in New York, he had trouble talking coaches into the idea. The coaches decided the heavy-legged youngster was built to be a middle linebacker. It did not take long to realize their mistake, however, and Csonka was put in as fullback beside Floyd Little. Little, who later starred with the Denver Broncos, won most of the headlines. But Csonka showed enough power to catch the pros' attention. The Miami Dolphins wasted no time in choosing him in the first round of the 1968 draft.

During those first years with Miami, Larry's strange running style nearly ended his career. He liked to run with both arms wrapped around the ball, which meant he didn't have a free arm for

Larry Csonka

catching himself when he fell. After one hard fall on his head, Csonka blacked out. He began to get such terrible headaches that some doctors thought he should quit football. But once he learned to carry the ball in one arm, the headaches stopped. Just to be safe, Larry always kept his helmet tipped so far forward it almost covered his eyes.

By 1971 Csonka was nearly unstoppable. That

year he topped 1,000 yards for the first time. In 1972 his crunching runs helped Miami to a perfect 17-0 record and a Super Bowl win. The next season was the third straight in which he ran over 1,000 yards. His running in the Super Bowl game that year proved he belonged with the great runners of all time. Larry simply ran over the Minnesota Vikings. He moved the ball so well that Miami only threw seven passes. With 145 yards gained and two touchdowns, Larry was named the Super Bowl's Most Valuable Player in the 24-7 win.

The only thing that saved opponents from more of Larry's bruising runs was a new league. In 1975 Larry signed with Memphis of the World Football League. He made more money than yardage in the new league, but by midseason the league had gone out of business. For the first time in years, Csonka spent the late autumn season on his farm.

The New York Giants thought Larry was just the man to make them into a winning team in 1976. They signed him to a contract and waited for him to "tear up" the league again. But it never happened. With poor blocking, Larry never got going. Even though they had paid a huge price for him, the Giants dropped him from the team in 1978.

After brief stays with the World Football League and the New York Giants, Larry returned to the Miami Dolphins in 1979.

Few experts thought Csonka could still play well. But his old coach at Miami, Don Shula, did not give up on him. Shula was tired of fumbles that cost his team a play-off win. He knew Csonka could hold on to the football, so he gave him his old job back. But even Shula was a little suprised at Csonka's success. Larry ground out 837 yards and scored 12 touchdowns as Miami won their divisional title. It seemed just like old times!

Of course Larry was more than a battering ram. If all it took were size and muscles to gain yards, every team would have their largest people running the ball. Instead Larry, who retired in 1980, was able to find openings in the blocking wall. Unlike many backs, he did not waste time looking for a chance at a long run. He was just as content to gain three tough yards through a pile of defenders. And although he broke his nose more times than he could count while getting those tough yards, Larry would tell you it was all part of the fun of football.

New York Jet John Riggins runs over New York Giant tacklers.

3
John Riggins

It's easy to get the wrong idea about John Riggins. A first look at his 230-pound body might make a coach think he is a power runner. Just by looking at his size a coach wouldn't think of letting this man try to outrun smaller defenders on end runs. Coaches who have used John as a bulldozer were sure to get a few yards straight ahead, but such plays were a waste of his talent.

While John may look like a Csonka-type runner, one of his best weapons is his speed. He is the fastest of the big fullbacks. When he goes full speed in the open field, he is likely to run all the way to the end zone.

Born in the small town of Centralia, Kansas, in 1949, John began running almost as soon as he could walk. In high school, he set a Kansas state record with a time of 6.4 in the 60-yard dash.

When he traveled with his high school track team, opponents may have expected him to put the shot because of his large size. But big John came with his running shoes. He proved himself to be the fastest schoolboy in Kansas by winning the state finals in the 100-yard dash two years in a row.

After high school, Riggins stayed close to home. In 1967 he started at the University of Kansas. While there, John never missed a football game or a practice. Exciting runner Gale Sayers had first gained headlines at Kansas. But by the time John finished at Kansas in 1971, it was he, and not Sayers, who owned most of the school's running records.

The New York Jets were looking for a fullback that year. They surprised many of their fans by choosing Riggins over John Brockington of Ohio State. But the Jets liked to throw the ball more than most teams and figured Riggins was a better pass blocker and pass receiver than Brockington. The Jets had made a wise choice. In his first year, Riggins led the team in both running and pass-catching.

It was overwhelming for John, a small-town boy, to become a star in New York City. He was thrilled

In 1976 Riggins became a free agent and joined the Washington Redskins.

just to see his name and picture on a bubble gum card. And the size of New York City amazed John as much as his stardom did. He could hardly believe all the traffic. In fact, he thought the roughest part of pro football was driving to the stadium. John was a lot more comfortable avoiding tacklers on the field than he had been avoiding cars on the streets.

The Jets' passing attack made it hard for their runners to gain yards. Their linemen's main job was to protect the star quarterback, Joe Namath. They blocked much better on pass plays than for runs. But John had his ways of getting attention. He formed a one-man war party to give his team a good running attack. He shaved his head like a Mohawk Indian—bald on the sides with a long strip of hair down the middle—and he went out to fight for every yard he could get. In five years with New York, John gained nearly 4,000 yards.

In 1976 Riggins became one of pro football's first "free agent" stars and said goodbye to the big city. A free agent is one who plays for a year without signing a contract. After that he is free to play for whatever team wants him the most. It did not seem to make much sense when John decided to join the Washington Redskins. Their blockers were not much better than the Jets. For two years, Riggins must have wondered about his choice, too. Used mainly as a power runner, he gained few yards. In 1977 injuries held him down to only 203 yards running.

But in 1978 the Redskins let Riggins roam the open spaces. With a chance to run end sweeps and

Washington's John Riggins cuts behind a Redskin blocker.

draw plays, John gained 1,104 yards. This earned him pro football's Comeback Player of the Year award.

John had his best year ever in 1979. He gained 1,153 yards and scored 12 touchdowns. By the end of the season, he was the ninth-leading rusher of all time, and he was moving up quickly.

In their last game in 1979, Washington needed a win over the Dallas Cowboys to make the playoffs. Late in the game, Riggins escaped from the Cowboy defenders and sprinted toward his right. Down the sideline he raced with Dallas's fastest defensive backs on his heels. No one could catch the nine-year veteran as he galloped 66 yards to score. Though the Redskins lost the game, John showed a large number of football fans how fast he could move.

In 1980 John had contract problems with the Redskin management. Because John and Washington couldn't agree on how much he should get paid, John sat out the entire season. By 1981 the future of John's career was uncertain. If John decides to retire, however, one thing *is* certain: pro football will not find too many 230-pound running backs with the speed and breakaway quickness that John had.

4
Franco Harris

Franco Harris is one football star who does not spend the off-season hiding from fans. He can afford to live anywhere he chooses, but he makes his home in the middle of a busy Pittsburgh neighborhood in a house built in the 1800s. Franco enjoys the city of Pittsburgh. And Pittsburgh is wild about Franco. Harris's fans, including "Franco's Italian Army," make sure he does not go unnoticed. They know Franco is the workhorse running back of their champion team, the Pittsburgh Steelers.

Franco Harris was born in Mt. Holly, New Jersey, in 1950. His mother is from Italy, which explains his unusual first name. His father is a black American who has spent most of his life working for the U.S. Army. Franco grew up shining shoes at the army base in New Jersey.

Franco's high school football coaches remember him as a fine runner. But some thought he was almost "too nice" for such a rough sport. After a game, Franco even went out of his way to shake hands with the defenders who had gone out of their way to hurt him.

In 1968 Harris went off to Penn State University. There he teamed up with another New Jersey high school star, Lydell Mitchell. The two of them started in Penn State's backfield for three years. Being a quarterback for Penn State was a dull job then. With Harris and Mitchell running with the ball, there was rarely any reason to pass!

Franco worked especially hard during his last year of college. He wanted the pro scouts to notice him. But an injury forced him to miss some games early in the year. During that time, Lydell Mitchell played some terrific games. When Franco returned to action, he spent most of his time blocking for Mitchell, who later starred with the Baltimore Colts.

Franco nearly wrecked his pro chances during practice for the 1971 Cotton Bowl. Twice he showed up late for workouts. As punishment, he was taken out of the starting lineup. Harris was afraid the pros would think he was undependable, but the

Franco Harris

Pittsburgh Steelers used their first choice to draft the quick 235-pounder.

In 1972 the Steelers looked forward to seeing their new star in action. In training camp, though, they were horrified by what they saw. On the field, Harris looked like a child who had gotten lost in a crowd. He seemed timid and easy to tackle.

But by the sixth game of the year, injuries had

put most of the other Steeler runners on the sidelines and they needed Franco. As it turned out, Franco was just like a cold car in winter. It took him a while to get warmed up, but once he did, there was no stopping him. By the end of the year, he had gained over 1,000 yards and had helped to put Pittsburgh in the play-offs. After his incredible play-off catch to beat Oakland, Franco fans popped up everywhere in Pittsburgh.

Harris was slowed down by injuries the following year. But ever since then, he has made the Steelers' running attack one of football's best. He has reached the 1,000-yard mark six years in a row.

Unlike most power runners, Franco stands straight up when he runs instead of leaning forward. Because of this, he is a master at changing directions quickly. On many of his best plays, Harris takes a quick toss from the quarterback and dashes toward the side of the field. Because defenders know he is quick enough to scoot around the defense, they race toward the sideline to cut him off. Then at the right moment, Franco stops and turns upfield. Defenders have trouble stopping and try to grab onto him with their arms. But Franco brushes off arm tackles as if they were dandruff!

Running behind a Steeler blocker, Franco looks for an opening to burst through.

Franco's running style is also one reason why he is at his best in play-off games. Play-off weather in Pittsburgh is often miserable, and the field is usually frozen. While others have trouble keeping their feet under them, Harris' straight-up style of

33

running keeps his center of balance away from his feet, and he never seems to slip. Franco doesn't seem to realize that ice is supposed to be slippery!

The Steelers' bearded fullback was at his best in the 1975 Super Bowl. He hauled the football 158 yards in 34 tries against the tough Minnesota Vikings' defense. Both marks are Super Bowl records. Because his was the only outstanding offense shown by either team in a 16-6 win, Franco easily won the Most Valuable Player Award. He has also scored touchdowns in both the 1979 and 1980 Super Bowl games.

Most running backs dream of gaining 1,000 yards in a season. Others would give anything to win a Super Bowl. Franco Harris owns *four* Super Bowl rings and has had *seven* 1,000-yard years. Another runner's dream is just an ordinary year's work for this workhorse of the Steelers.

5
Greg Pruitt

Even before the oil shortages, Greg Pruitt was not one to waste energy. His running energy, that is. Greg is too valuable a runner to be ramming into the line on carry after carry. Instead he is called on when the Cleveland Browns need a long gain. Just one of his darting 70-yard runs can mean the difference between winning and losing. Though he does not run the ball as often as bigger backs, he has no trouble keeping up with them. His total of over 4,000 yards gained in four years—from 1975 to 1978—is one of the best in the pros.

Greg was born in Houston, Texas, in 1951. He was small when he was born and grew to be only 5 feet, 9 inches, and 190 pounds—not the ideal of the "tall Texan." Every day of his career, Greg has been about the smallest man on the field. On his first day of football practice in the 7th grade, Greg looked around at his teammates.

Not one of them was as short as he, but he was determined that being small would not stop him. Yet even fine seasons at Elmore High in Houston did not convince many college coaches that Greg could help their teams.

Greg's size didn't stop the University of Oklahoma from thinking he was a good player. But when Greg started school there, the coaches wanted to make a pass receiver out of him so he could use his speed to stay clear of the big guys. But the problem was that catching wasn't Greg's strong point.

Around the time Greg was playing for Oklahoma, college teams began to use the wishbone offense. This offense needed one strong fullback, a tricky quarterback, and a fast halfback. On each play, the quarterback had a choice of handing-off to the fullback, of running himself, or of flipping the ball to the halfback. If he were clever, the defense would not know who would end up with the ball. Pruitt seemed the ideal person for the halfback spot.

Oklahoma's wishbone offense rolled over its opponents in 1971. The running plays worked so well that the team almost never passed. Greg's end runs were astounding. With an open field to

Greg Pruitt

run in and only three or four men to dodge, he was unstoppable. He became one of the few college runners in history to gain almost 200 yards a game. And to reach that total it only took him half the carries it took other stars!

When Oklahoma played Nebraska in 1971 and 1972, it was the biggest show in college football.

Not only were two top teams playing, but "super midgets" Greg Pruitt and Johnny Rodgers of Nebraska were battling for the Heisman Trophy. In 1972, after what must have been a hard decision, Rodgers received the trophy instead of Pruitt.

Greg was a cheerful chatterbox who talked a lot about what he could do as a runner. He did a lot of bragging to get some attention from the pros. Although he was tearing up the turf, Greg was hearing some familiar stories from pro scouts, who usually overlook small players. "Pruitt's a great runner. Too bad he's so small," they said. "Maybe he'll do better as a wide receiver."

But the Cleveland Browns could not help looking at Pruitt's record. How many men in college average almost a first down every time they run? They chose Greg on the second round of the 1973 draft.

Like many rookie runners, Greg started out running back kicks. His jackrabbit starts and stops left the defensive line spinning. In his first three years, he gained over 2,000 yards in returns, including a few touchdowns for the Browns. But Greg wasn't satisfied. He told the Browns he was tough enough to start at running back.

Sure enough, in 1975 Greg proved even more

With blinding speed and dazzling moves, Greg is a threat to run for a touchdown on every play.

dangerous at running back. He darted through defenses like a waterbug and often used his shortness to his advantage. Greg would hide behind blockers until a tackler moved to one side or the other. Then he would go the opposite way.

Pruitt is always careful to stay away from head-on collisions with large linemen. Even so, during

Despite his small size, Greg is one of the most explosive running backs in football.

most of his career he has had trouble with nagging injuries, most of them to his ankles. But in spite of his injuries, Pruitt has managed to pile up impressive records. In 1975, 1976, and 1977, Pruitt gained over 1,000 yards. In just one game against Kansas City in 1975, he gained 214 yards. In 1978, even though he missed several games because of injuries, Pruitt averaged 5.5 yards per carry and just missed the 1,000-yard mark by 60 yards.

The records show Pruitt again led the Browns in rushing in 1979 with over 1,000 yards. But it wasn't Greg, it was Mike Pruitt. Greg spent a frustrating year sitting out with serious leg problems. Mike, who is not related to Greg, was one of the Browns' top draft choices in 1977. After the success they have had with Greg, who can blame the Browns for wanting another Pruitt running the ball? For when Greg Pruitt has been totally healthy, he has been called the greatest open-field runner since Gale Sayers.

Chuck Foreman was once the Minnesota Vikings' most powerful weapon. He could either dance around or run right through the opposition.

6
Chuck Foreman

Chuck Foreman probably learned very little about playing running back from his boyhood heroes, linemen such as Alex Karras and John Mackey. Chuck's older brother, Fran, was an offensive lineman with the Buffalo Bills for a short time in 1970. So it is not surprising that young Chuck spent his time learning to block and tackle. In fact, by the time he joined the pros, Chuck still had not spent much time running with the football.

Walter Eugene Foreman, nicknamed "Chuck" by his mother, was born and raised in Frederick, Maryland. Even when he was a small boy, it was easy to see that Chuck belonged on a football field. In fact, he was such a fine all-around player that coaches didn't know the right spot for him.

Chuck was big and strong enough to play defensive tackle in high school. He could also catch passes and block so he played tight end on offense. But after entering the University of Miami (Florida) in 1969, Foreman showed other skills. He was a sure tackler, so he was put at defensive back. But then he ran the ball so well that Miami tried him at halfback. And as a halfback, his running proved even fast enough for him to play wide receiver. The easygoing Foreman put up with all this shuffling and somehow seemed to do better at each new position. In his last year of college, he was doing more pass-catching than running.

Foreman showed enough skill to earn a spot in two All-Star games in 1972. Moved back to running back, he won the Most Valuable Player Award in both the North-South game and the Senior Bowl.

In 1973 the Minnesota Vikings drafted Foreman and solved the problem of where to play him. Rather than have him chase around at different positions, they kept him in one place. But even though he was listed as a running back, he was really much more. The 6-foot, 2-inch, 212-pound runner could tear into the line or dash around the ends. He sprinted far downfield for long passes and

Chuck Foreman

out-jumped linebackers for short ones. If the Vikings needed a yard for a touchdown or a first down, Chuck would get it for them. On those important plays he tumbled high over the clogged line of scrimmage to get the yard.

In the mid-1970s, Foreman was the man every team wished they had. He was like having two or three star players rolled into one. In 1973 Chuck was named Rookie of the Year, and in each of his first two years, 1973 and 1974, he helped the Vikings get to the Super Bowl.

In 1975 Foreman moved the ball more yards and in more ways than anyone else. He led the conference in pass-receiving with 73 grabs and in scoring with 22 touchdowns. He ran for 1,070 more yards. If he had gained just 6 more yards he would have been the first player to lead the league in all three areas! Still he was not named the conference's Most Valuable Player that year, an award he had won in 1974 and would win again in 1976.

In 1976 Chuck gained a career-high total of 1,155 yards running. In the National Football Conference championship that year, Minnesota and the Los Angeles Rams were fighting to a draw in the second half. Suddenly Chuck roared through an opening on the Rams' left side. He faked out a Ram defender and raced 57 yards to set up the winning score.

Some announcers have called Chuck "Plastic Man." As he twists and turns to fake out defenders, his body seems to be made of plastic. In Chuck's best years, the first man with a chance to tackle him often tackled nothing but air. Though he has had many chances, Foreman does not believe in making a big show after a touchdown. He quietly hands the ball to an official and lets his running get the attention.

In 1978 the Vikings' blocking fell apart. Even with Foreman, they became the poorest running team in football. By the next season the blocking had improved, but Foreman fell apart. One year before, he had been one of football's brightest stars. But in 1979, he dropped passes and eked out only 215 yards. Minnesota fans were sure it was all over for Chuck. They knew a top running back's career can end suddenly. It had happened before to such players as John Brockington, Larry Brown, and Jim Nance.

In 1980 Chuck was traded to the New England Patriots. He hoped a fresh start with the Patriots, a fine blocking team, would help him to regain his form.

But Chuck did not do well with the Patriots. He gained only 63 yards in 23 carries and was released before the 1981 season.

Meanwhile, the task of replacing Foreman was not an easy one for the Vikings. It was hard to make up for the loss of the star player who led them in running, receiving, and scoring in their Super Bowl years.

Walter Payton of the Chicago Bears breaks away from two Green Bay Packer defenders.

7
Walter Payton

At 5 feet, 11 inches, and 205 pounds, Walter Payton is fairly small for a pro running back. Yet defensive players do not think of him as small. Even Walter does not seem to realize he is smaller than most players. He likes to battle defenders head on, as well as outrun them.

Walter was born in Columbia, Mississippi, in 1954. As a boy, he did not miss many chances to use his great leg strength. He set school long-jump records, starred in gymnastics, and even whirled his way to a second-place finish in a national dance contest.

Payton played football at Jackson State University, a small college in Mississippi. It didn't take him long to become their star runner. Opponents quickly discovered that Walter was attracted to end zones like a magnet. By the end of his college career, he had crossed the goal line 66 times.

Off the football field, Payton was usually quiet and serious. But there were times when he would play tricks that gave his teammates fits. One night before a game, he called up his coach. Using a different voice he told the coach that the team's quarterback had been arrested. The poor coach was up half the night worrying about his quarterback. Of course there had been no arrest. When it came to studies, though, Walter was all business. It usually takes a person four years to graduate from college, but Walter finished in three years.

Pro football scouts have always kept their eyes on players from Jackson. Since this small college has turned out many fine pro football stars, the Chicago scouts were delighted when Walter joined their struggling team in 1975. The Bear veterans were also impressed with this polite, religious rookie, and nicknamed him "Sweetness." They were even more impressed by his running. Even though Payton only gained 679 yards his first year, his teammates could tell he was going to be something special.

Walter Payton

Some called his running style "crazy." They did not mean it was a bad way to run. They were talking about the furious way he spun in and out of tacklers' arms. As he bounced off tacklers, he sometimes seemed like a bumper car out of control.

In his second year, Payton began to take some headlines away from Buffalo's O. J. Simpson. Walter led the league in running most of the season, and Simpson had to hustle in the last few games to beat Payton for the rushing title.

In 1977 Walter completely took over as football's best runner. One game against the Minnesota Vikings had erased all doubt. Payton had come down with the flu before the contest, but because it was an important game for the Bears, he tried to play anyway. Walter certainly looked healthy to the Vikings that day. He ran over and through the defense for 275 yards—the most yards running anyone has ever gained in a single game. Payton finished that season with a total of 1,852 yards to lead the league. *The Sporting News* called him the top player in the league. Opponents could not decide which was harder: trying to stop Payton or trying to think of words to describe him!

Walter became such a fine runner that the Bears could hardly stand the thought of giving the ball to anyone else. After a while, defenses chased Walter whether he had the ball or not. With defenses swarming around him, the yards became tougher to get. But Walter would never go down without battling for all he could get. Although his extra effort usually paid off in extra yards, the results were sometimes embarrassing. During a Thanksgiving Day game in 1979, Walter lost his pants in the grasp of a Detroit Lion tackler!

Walter leaves Viking tacklers grabbing nothing but air.

Walter likes to keep charging ahead because he feels it's the best way to stay away from injuries. He believes runners who stand still or dance around are more likely to get hurt. Payton is also an expert at using his arm to brush away tacklers. And he doesn't mind letting his blockers share in the fun of scoring. After each of his touchdowns, he hands the ball to a lineman, who enjoys a chance to slam the ball against the ground.

Payton has other interests besides football. In fact he often says football is more like work than a game to him. Payton is near a master's degree in working with deaf and retarded people. But when it comes to running with the football, he is already a master.

8
Tony Dorsett

Every year from 1972 to 1976, the Dallas Cowboys came close to being pro football's best team. But they were never able to find the one thing they really needed: a good, fast running back. Opponents shuddered to think how good the Cowboys would have been if they had ever found one.

In the spring of 1977 it finally happened. Dallas traded four high-draft choices to the Seattle Seahawks for the right to draft Tony Dorsett. It was the worst news that Cowboys' rivals could have imagined. Not only was Dorsett fast, he was the best runner in the history of college football. Many people had the feeling there would be no stopping the Cowboy attack in 1977.

Since joining Dallas in 1977, Tony Dorsett has frustrated many Cowboy opponents—including this Redskin tackler.

Tony Drew Dorsett was born near Aliquippa, Pennsylvania, in 1954. His family and friends called him "Hawk" because of his large eyes. Like many men of the area, Tony's father was a steelworker. And like most boys in the town, Tony loved football. He tried to keep up with his three older brothers as they practiced on the playground. He soon found he could do more than just keep up. By high school, people were saying his initials, "T. D." were short for "Touchdown." He had visits from hundreds of college coaches, all begging him to attend their schools.

Since Tony wanted to stay close to home, he went to the University of Pittsburgh. It had been many years since Pittsburgh was a top football school. For the past ten years, they had had trouble finding *anyone* they could beat. They hoped one star player, such as Dorsett, could get them on the winning track again.

At first their new star was so shy he wouldn't talk. His teammates wondered if something were wrong with him. But there was certainly nothing wrong with his ball-carrying. Even as a freshman, Tony ripped through defenses for more than 100 yards a game. And sure enough, Pittsburgh began to win. Because of all the attention Tony was getting, other top players came to Pittsburgh.

The last game of Tony's college career was the Sugar Bowl on New Year's Day in 1977. A huge TV audience waited to see if the University of Georgia's "Junkyard Dog" defense could shut down the Pittsburgh flash. Not a chance! The 5-foot, 10-inch, 188-pound Dorsett zipped up and down the field for 202 yards. But even the Sugar Bowl game was just one small highlight in his career. During his last year at college and his first year as a pro, Tony put together two of the most incredible years in football history.

In 1976, his last year at the university, Tony led his team to the national college championship. He also won the Heisman Trophy, became the first runner in college history to gain over 6,000 yards, and broke 18 college football records.

The following year, his first year with the Dallas Cowboys, Tony gained over 1,000 yards, was named the conference Rookie of the Year, and scored a touchdown to help beat Denver in the Super Bowl.

Tony is the Cowboys' game breaker. He is so fast he can take the smallest bit of running room and turn it into a touchdown gallop. He can also change directions without losing speed, and he runs so smoothly and swiftly that at times he seems to be skating on ice.

With all this attention, Tony changed quite a bit from the shy freshman at the University of Pittsburgh. He spoke easily to the hundreds of reporters who hounded him all over the country, and he was not always modest when people asked him how well he would do. His boasting did not make him popular with coaches, players, and fans in Dallas. Then came other troubles. Cowboy coach Tom Landry benched him for missing a meeting, and fans began to boo him when he had trouble holding on to the ball. An injured toe in 1979 gave him even more problems.

Still Tony gained his yards. His 1,107 yard total in 1979 made him the second pro runner ever to gain over 1,000 yards in each of his first three seasons. Tony made these gains even though he did not get the ball as often as he would like because his teammate, Roger Staubach, was such a fine passer. But Staubach retired in 1980, and now Tony may have a chance to do more of the work. If he performs as well as he did in college, the record books may never be the same.

9
Wilbert Montgomery

The word has spread in the National Football League: "If you stop Wilbert Montgomery, you will beat the Philadelphia Eagles." It sounds like a simple plan. But stopping Montgomery has never been as easy as it might seem. This small, darting runner has averaged over four and one-half yards a carry since he started playing full time in 1978.

Perhaps the only way to slow down Wilbert is to let the defense bring microphones on the field. If there's one thing that makes Wilbert panic, it's reporters making a fuss over him. But he is such a big star in Philadelphia that he will just have to get used to the attention.

Wilbert, born in Greenville, Mississippi, in 1954, was one of nine children. But his was not always one big, happy family. His parents were divorced when Wilbert was 14. Wilbert stayed with his mother, Gladys, and worked for a bricklayer.

Wilbert came very close to missing a chance at a football career. After his older brother, Albert, hurt both shoulders playing college ball, Wilbert's mother would not allow her other boys to play.

But when Wilbert entered tenth grade, he started a "secret life" as a football star. He found someone to fake his mom's writing on a football permission slip and secretly went to practices and games. But because he was such a good player, it was not easy to keep the secret. He had to race home and hide the pictures of him that were in the sports section of the newspaper. Then college coaches began sending him letters. Wilbert had to meet the mailman to get those letters before his mom saw them.

After two years, Wilbert finally told his mother he was an all-state halfback at Greenville High. Since football would help him to pay for college, his mother let him continue playing.

Soon after Wilbert started playing football at Jackson State in 1973, he could see the backfield was crowded. With Walter Payton and Rickey Young (later a Minnesota Viking) as runners, the team needed no one else. So Wilbert moved on to Abilene Christian in Texas, where he scored 76 touchdowns in four years.

Wilbert Montgomery

    The pro scouts took a long look at Montgomery. The program listed him as 5 feet, 10 inches, and 190 pounds, but he certainly looked smaller. They were also aware that he had missed many games in his last three years of college because of injuries. The scouts finally decided Wilbert could not last long in the pros, and it was not until the sixth round of the 1977 draft that the Philadelphia Eagles decided he was worth a try.

Reporters had always made Wilbert nervous, but they were not the only ones. He was jumpy even around his teammates, and he was especially afraid of Eagles' coach, Dick Vermeil. The scared rookie made so many mistakes in practice that the Eagles almost dropped him from the team. But they found one thing he could do well—return kicks. He led the conference in kickoff returns in 1977 with a 26.9-yard average. He even raced 99 yards for a score against the New York Giants. Meanwhile Wilbert had made only 183 yards as a second-string running back.

But the next year he broke loose for 1,220 yards. He scored four touchdowns in a game against the Washington Redskins and had a fifth called back because of a penalty. In 1978 Wilbert helped the Eagles to their first winning season since 1966. Becoming a winner hadn't changed him a bit, though. When he was chosen to play in the NFL All-Star game, the Pro Bowl game, he was embarrassed about all the attention he received.

1979 proved that Montgomery *did* belong with the All-Stars. On three out of every four Eagle running plays, Wilbert was the man with the ball. Other teams were waiting for him, but he still got

Though small for a running back, Wilbert is tough to bring down.

his yards. He was fast and strong and popped through the tiniest of openings in the line. That year Wilbert finished with 1,529 yards and led Philadelphia to the play-offs once again. His average of 4.5 yards per carry was one of the best among the top running backs.

Some of his blockers claim that Wilbert is so short the tacklers simply lose sight of him. Montgomery just wishes that *more* people would lose sight of him. In fact, during the off-seasons he manages to

A New York Giant pursues Wilbert as he tries to run around end.

hide so well that even the Eagles don't know how to reach him. But Wilbert knows when the new season starts, the reporters will be back. As long as he keeps gaining all those yards, people will want to talk to him. There is no such thing as a "secret star" in the National Football League.

Earl Campbell of the Houston Oilers is the most punishing runner in football.

10
Earl Campbell

B. C. and Anne Campbell bought an old farmhouse in Tyler, Texas, in 1966. A few months later, B. C. died suddenly of a heart attack, and Anne was left to raise 11 children by herself. The little money she made was earned by growing and selling roses. All of the children took their turns in the rose garden. But one of the boys, Earl, was not as much help as the others.

Mrs. Campbell made sure all of her children were in church every Sunday. But even that did not help to keep Earl out of trouble. He liked to pal around with a rough crowd in high school. They drank and smoked and skipped classes. Earl even quit going to football practice.

Mrs. Campbell saw what was happening to Earl. She told him it wasn't fair to fool around when the rest of the family had to work so hard. If he ever got put in jail, she said, there would be no money from her to bail him out. Earl finally got the message. He settled down and worked hard.

One of the smartest things Earl did was rejoin the Tyler High School football team. He did well enough to earn a scholarship to the University of Texas. It did not take long for word to spread among the colleges: Campbell was not only fast, he was also a hitter. At 5 feet, 11 inches, and 225 pounds, he was not afraid to knock heads. In 1977 he won the Heisman Trophy as the nation's top college football player.

The Houston Oilers went to a lot of trouble to see that this prize Texas star did not leave the state. They traded starting tight end Jimmie Giles and four draft choices to the Tampa Bay Buccaneers for the right to draft Earl. From the first day of practice, Earl showed his teammates he was worth the price.

Before Earl arrived in 1978, Houston had had little offense. They had depended on quarterback Dan Pastorini to throw long passes and hoped the

Earl runs through the Oilers' arch rival—the Pittsburgh Steelers.

right person caught the ball. Few teams can win many games on such gambles. But Campbell gave the Oilers an instant running attack. Defenders could not stay back and wait for Pastorini to throw. Now their first job was to stop Campbell.

Most defenders were in for a nasty shock the first time they tackled Earl. No one in football runs into people full blast as hard as Earl does. Campbell has sent many unprepared linebackers flying head over heels. Most experts thought Earl should take better care of himself. They did not see how anyone could survive such bone-jarring crashes for very long—especially since Houston gave him the ball 20 to 30 times every game! But Earl refused to slow down. He wanted to give his best on every play.

In one close game against the Miami Dolphins, Earl carried the ball time after time. By the fourth quarter, he was nearly worn out. But the Oilers were down on their own end of the field. Since they needed a first down, Earl took the handoff and set out to get a few important yards. By the time he was through, he had run past everyone for a long touchdown! In his very first year, Earl led the league with 1,450 yards, and the Oilers pointed to him as the reason they made the 1978 play-offs.

Earl was even better the next year. In one of his best games, he gained over 100 yards against the Pittsburgh Steelers' famous defense. His total of 1,697 yards gained again led the league. Campbell's 19 touchdowns were also tops in the league. Again, Houston made the final round of the American Football Conference play-offs.

Earl Campbell

One big play the Oilers enjoyed executing during 1979 was on fourth down with a yard to go for a first down. Usually those plays are dangerous gambles for the offense. It's usually safer to punt the ball. But with Earl in the backfield, there hardly seems to be any risk at all!

Houston feels Earl is just as important as a good example as he is as a player. No one can remember ever hearing him complain. And even with all his fame, Earl is modest. He works hard and cares a lot about other people, especially his mother. He is just as proud of his mother as she is of him and does not miss a chance to give his mother credit for helping him to become the kind of person he is. Earl has built his mother a new house right next to their old farm house in Tyler. Houston fans, too, give Mrs. Campbell a lot of credit for raising a fine son like Earl and shower her with as much attention as Earl. A sign often seen in the Houston Astrodome reads, "Thank you, Mrs. Campbell." And the cheers that echo around the stadium show how they feel about her son—the man who carried their team to three straight play-offs.

ACKNOWLEDGMENTS: The photographs are reproduced through the courtesy of: pp. 4, 56, Dallas Cowboys; pp. 8, 11, Buffalo Bills, Robert L. Smith Photo; p. 13, O. J. Simpson Enterprises; pp. 16, 18, 20, Miami Dolphins; p. 22, New York Jets; p. 25, Washington Redskins; p. 27, Washington Redskins, Nate Fine Photo; pp. 31, 33, Pittsburgh Steelers; p. 37, Cleveland Browns, Henry M. Barr Studio, Inc.; pp. 39, 40, Cleveland Browns; pp. 42, 45, Minnesota Vikings; pp. 48, 51, 53, Chicago Bears; pp. 62, 64, 65, Philadelphia Eagles; pp. 66, 69, 71, Houston Oilers.

Cover photograph: Vernon J. Biever